Mapping the World

VOLUME 1

WAYS OF MAPPING THE WORLD

GROLIER
EDUCATIONAL

Published 2002 by Grolier Educational, Danbury, CT 06816

This edition published exclusively for the school and library market

Produced by Andromeda Oxford Limited
11–13 The Vineyard, Abingdon,
Oxon OX14 3PX, U.K.

Copyright © Andromeda Oxford Limited 2002

Contributors: *Peter Evea, Stella Douglas, Peter Elliot, David Fairbairn, Ian Falconer*

Project Consultant: *Dr. David Fairbairn, Lecturer in Geomatics, University of Newcastle-upon-Tyne, England*

Project Director: *Graham Bateman*
Managing Editor: *Shaun Barrington*
Design Manager: *Frankie Wood*
Editorial Assistant: *Marian Dreier*
Picture Researcher: *David Pratt*
Picture Manager: *Claire Turner*
Production: *Clive Sparling*
Index: *Janet Dudley*

Design and origination by Gecko

Printed in Hong Kong

Set ISBN 0-7172-5619-7

Library of Congress Cataloging-in-Publication Data

Mapping the world.
   p. cm.
Includes index.
Contents: v. 1. Ways of mapping the world -- v. 2. Observation and measurement -- v. 3. Maps for travelers -- v. 4. Navigation -- v. 5. Mapping new lands -- v. 6. Mapping for governments -- v. 7. City maps -- v. 8. Mapping for today and tomorrow.
ISBN 0-7172-5619-7 (set : alk. paper)
   1. Cartography -- Juvenile literature. [1. Cartogaphy. Maps.] I. Grolier Educational (Firm)

GA105.6 .M37 2002
562 -- dc21

                                        2001051229

Contents

About This Set

Mapping the World is an eight-volume set that describes the history of cartography, discusses its importance in the development of different cultures, and explains how it is done. Cartography is the technique of compiling information for, and then drawing, maps or charts. Each volume examines a particular aspect of mapping and is illustrated by numerous artworks and photographs selected to help understanding of the sometimes complex themes.

After all, cartography is both a science and an art. It has existed since before words were written down and today uses the most up-to-date computer technology and imaging systems. It is vital to governments in peacetime and in wartime, as much as to the individual business person, geologist, vacationer–or pirate! Advances in mapmaking through history have been closely involved with wider advances in science and technology. It demands some understanding of math and at the same time an appreciation of visual creativity. Such a subject is bound to get a little complex at times!

What Is a Map?

We all think we know, but the word is surprisingly difficult to define. "A representation of the earth, or part of the earth, or another part of the universe–usually on a flat surface–that shows a group of features in terms of their relative size and position." But even this long-winded attempt is not the whole story: As explained in Volume 1, most early cultures tried to map the unseen–the underworld, the realms of gods, or the unknown structure of the cosmos. Maps are not just ink on paper or lines on a computer screen. They can be "mental maps." And the problem of mapping a round object–the earth or one of the planets–on a flat surface means that there is no perfect flat map, one that shows precise "size and position."

The cartographer has to compromise to show relative location, direction, and area in the best way

for a specific purpose. He or she must decide what information to include and what to leave out: A sea chart is very different from a subway map. This set explains how the information is gathered–by surveying, for example–and how the cartographer makes decisions about scale, map projection, symbols, and all other aspects of mapmaking.

Researching a Subject

Separate topics in the set are presented in sections of from two to six pages so that your understanding of the subject grows in a logical way. Words and phrases in *italic* are explained more fully in the glossaries. Each glossary is specific to one volume. There is a set index in each volume. Recommended further reading and websites are also listed in each volume. At the bottom of each left-hand page there are cross-references to other sections in the set that expand on some aspect of the subject under discussion.

By consulting the index and cross-references, you can follow a particular topic across the set volumes. Each volume takes a different approach. For example, different aspects of the work of the famous mapmaker Gerardus Mercator are discussed in several volumes: the mathematical basis of his map projection in Volume 2, his importance for navigation in Volume 4, and his success as a businessman in Volume 5.

The continuous effort to improve mapping is part of the history of exploration, navigation, warfare, politics, and technology. All of these subjects–and many more–are discussed in *Mapping the World*.

Maps and artworks help explain technical points in the text

Cross-references to other relevant sections in the set give section title, volume number, and page references

Introduction to Volume 1

How do we start to make a map? Each person's view of the world is different, and that means that many different maps are created. This volume considers how human beings have looked at the world in the past and the maps they have produced. The use of photographs of the earth, especially from the air, has made maps more accurate and standardized, but there are still possibilities for new maps to be made by creative people. Maps do not just show features in the landscape: It is important to understand the difference between topographic and thematic maps.

Summary introduces the section topic

Main entry heading to a two-, four-, or six-page section

Each volume is color-coded

Photographs and illustrations of people, locations, instruments–and, of course, maps–add to the text information

Aspects of the section subject are sometimes explained in separate information boxes

▶ Calculating Longitude

For a long time sailors were able to work out their latitude, or position relative to the equator. While explorers kept in sight of the coast, there was little need to calculate how far they had traveled in an easterly or westerly direction. However, as explorers traveled further away from home, they needed more and more to know their longitude.

Lines of longitude, called *meridians*, are imaginary lines on the earth's surface running directly from the North Pole to the South Pole. Longitude is measured eastward and westward from the Prime Meridian (0°). In 1884 an international agreement fixed this line to run through Greenwich in London, England. The longitude of a point is the angle at the center of the earth between the meridian on which it lies and the Prime Meridian. The degrees are numbered west and east of Greenwich up to 180°.

Establishing position in an east-west direction was historically much more difficult than working out a ship's latitude, and for centuries sailors could do no more than estimate their longitude, often not very accurately, using dead reckoning (see page 11).

Early methods of trying to measure longitude involved noting the distances of certain stars from the moon or observing the orbits of Jupiter's moons, but none was accurate enough. It is possible to calculate longitude by using the position of the stars. However, the problem with this method is that the stars shift their position eastward every day. To use their positions to calculate your own position, you need to know the precise local time relative to a fixed reference point.

The earth turns 360° (a complete revolution) every day and 15° every hour. If a navigator knew the time in Greenwich, England, which is on the Prime Meridian, or 0° of longitude, and also knew the precise local time, it would be simple math to multiply the time difference (in hours) by 15 to give

John Harrison 1693–1776

In 1714 the British Board of Longitude announced a competition. Whoever could invent a method for accurately finding a ship's longitude would win a huge prize of £20,000. The government was not giving away such a large amount of money for nothing. Being able to calculate longitude could provide enormous advantages in international trading and military seapower, to say nothing of helping prevent disasters at sea resulting from poor navigation. To win the prize, the ship's longitude had to be measured to an accuracy of 0.5 degrees, or 30 minutes, of longitude. Harrison knew that he could win if he could produce a very accurate marine clock, or chronometer. His fourth, brilliant design proved to be accurate enough to win the competition. It was tested at sea during 1761 and 1762, and experiments found that over a 5-month period it had an error of just 1.25 minutes of longitude, easily accurate enough to win the prize.

▶ ▲ Harrison with an earlier clock (above) and the compact design of his fourth model (left).

the ship's longitude. To do this, there had to be an accurate way of measuring time.

Johan Werner first suggested using some sort of timekeeper as early as 1514 but was not able to build one that had enough accuracy. Until John Harrison's designs clocks had to be constantly adjusted. And the problem was even worse at sea, with changes in temperature, dampness, and the ship's movement all upsetting a clock's delicate mechanism. Harrison succeeded in overcoming all these problems. His development of the marine chronometer in the 18th century finally allowed navigators to accurately determine their longitude. By referring to nautical almanacs that were compiled by astronomical observatories, the navigators could work out their position east or west as well as north or south.

◀ World time zones. The time changes by one hour for every 15° of longitude traveled around the earth. You lose or gain a day crossing the International Date Line.

Time Zones

Because the earth spins by 15° of longitude every hour, anyone traveling in a westerly direction will lengthen the day by one hour for every 15° of longitude traveled. Similarly, traveling eastward will shorten the day by one hour. This distance is a long way at the equator, but less and less the further south or north you are. A sailor could not continue to gain or lose time for ever, so in 1884 a Canadian engineer called Sir Sandford Fleming suggested a system of time zones (see diagram on page 20).

He also proposed the International Date Line. This line runs north-south through the Pacific Ocean and avoids major landmasses. When a traveler crosses the line going westward (say, flying from Los Angeles to Sydney), a day is added. Nine on the morning of June 10 immediately becomes 9 a.m. on June 11. In the opposite direction (for example, from Auckland in New Zealand to Honolulu) 9 a.m. on June 11 becomes 9 a.m. on June 10.

SEE ALSO: LATITUDE, LONGITUDE, AND POSITIONING **2**: 26–29, FINDING YOUR WAY ON THE OCEAN **1**: 10–11

Captions explain context of illustrations

20

21

The Earth from Space

Long before human beings ventured into space-long before the invention of aircraft-they had begun to think of the earth as viewed from above. That allowed them to represent objects, places, and the distances between them on a flat surface: on a map.

Imagine being an astronaut: looking down at our blue-green planet from an orbiting spacecraft. The scenes you see might be very complex–images of intricate coastlines and varying patterns of vegetation. In some places you might be able to see the effect of human beings on our planet. You could probably spot clearings in the South American rain forest. There might be pollution clouds in the air from factories. Perhaps a large man-made reservoir would reflect the sunlight. At night you could see the pattern of lights showing where mankind has settled and built towns and cities.

All of these features of the earth's surface can be measured and put on maps. Even features in the atmosphere, like cloud patterns, and things on the seabed (invisible to us on dry land) can be measured and presented on a map. A map is the best way of storing all this information about the earth. To help make sense of the complicated world we live in, people have used maps for centuries.

Looking Down

Very early in human history people had the idea of making markings on a small object–perhaps a rock or part of a cave wall–act as a description of a large area. The lines and pictures drawn on these small objects were representing a very big object–sometimes even

SEE ALSO: TRYING TO EXPLAIN THE UNIVERSE WITH MAPS 1: 22–25; LATITUDE, LONGITUDE, AND POSITIONING 2: 26–29

the whole world. Early people were able, just as we are today, to have a picture of the world in their mind. It could help them in remembering what was over the next hilltop, or it could be their view of what the world as a whole might look like—though they could not see or measure it as we can. They could draw that picture as a map.

Maps are particular views of the world, and one of their special characteristics is that they are views from above, looking downward. That is a surprising viewpoint for early humans to have because none of them could have seen the world, directly from the sky above. But it is important to imagine this viewpoint because making maps depends on it. To see large areas of the world, you need, really, to put yourself in the position of the astronaut. To see over the hill, you need to have the viewpoint of a bird.

Man-made Features

Astronauts who have traveled far away from earth are able to see a complete *hemisphere* (half the globe of the world) at one glance. However, because astronauts are so far away, they cannot see many individual features on the surface of the earth. Whole continents may be visible, but many of the features that make up the area you live in are not. Landscapes created by human beings—roads, buildings, and cities—are not features that astronauts can see.

The biggest features visible from space that are the results of human activities are the polders of the Netherlands in Europe. A polder is an area of land that has been reclaimed from the sea by draining it and by building walls to keep the sea out. The polders have allowed the country to increase its total land area by a fifth. This extra 800 square miles (2,000 sq km) of land is very important for the Netherlands, which has a high population. Though the sea often breaks through the walls and causes flooding.

It is only when you travel closer and closer to the earth from space that you are able to pick out other man-made objects—cities and land patterns in farming areas. Clearly, the closer you are to earth, the more features you can identify and include on a map.

◄ Looking down on the earth from the Hubble space telescope in orbit 320 miles (515 km) above. The pattern top right is not snow but clouds.

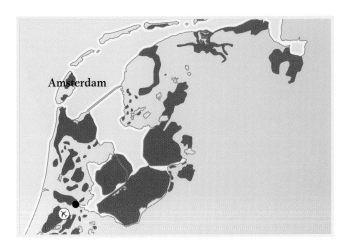

▲ The polders of the Netherlands. The drainage work has been carried out since medieval times and has transformed marshy areas, mud flats, and some shallow coastal waters into usable agricultural and settled land.

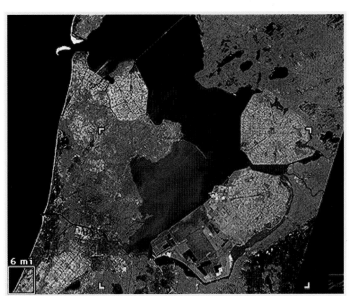

▲ The polders from space. The majority of the larger polders are used for agriculture, and the field patterns are noticeable from infared satellite images like this. More than $\frac{1}{3}$ of the Netherlands is below sea level.

Your Neighborhood from the Air

Almost all maps take a bird's-eye view of an area; they look down. Only "almost all," because star maps look up. (Though in fact some birds actually do look up, navigating by the stars!) Since the invention of the airplane, there has been a photographic method of using the bird's-eye view to produce maps.

Birds are able to fly to a maximum height of only a couple of miles before the air becomes too thin for them to stay up or even stay alive. But what a view the birds get when looking at the world from such a height! The birds that fly above your neighborhood are able to pick out your house and the surrounding streets, your school and the local shopping mall, the parks and trees. They are all objects that can be shown on a map.

From a commercial jet at maximum altitude, which can be six or seven miles above the earth, you can see mainly natural features such as forests, oceans and deserts. Maps that show whole countries include these features. As the airplane descends, more and more of the human world can be seen. Objects such as cities, highways that connect them, farms and their field patterns, harbors, and airports become visible. As you come down further, you reach a point where you get the same view as a bird. You can see the pattern of streets in the neighborhood and the individual buildings, and you notice the cars and the backyards.

▼ A photograph of a neighborhood in Fort Lauderdale, Florida, from the air looking almost straight down. Many features such as houses, trees, roads, and in this case, waterways can be seen.

SEE ALSO: *MEASURING FROM PHOTOGRAPHS* **2:** *22–25*

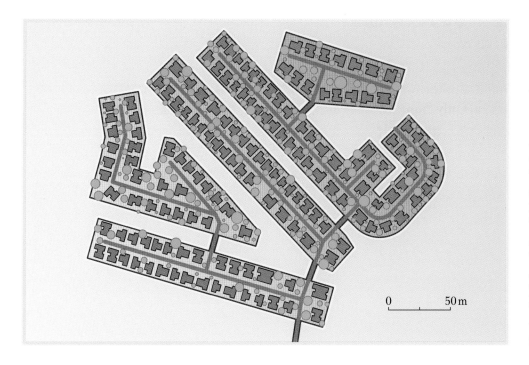

0   50 m

◄ The map of Fort Lauderdale is almost the same shape as the main area of the photograph opposite. But this is a "straight down" view with symbols showing trees, houses, roads, and bridges. The blue background is a deliberate color choice because—like the polders on page 7—this neighborhood has been built on "reclaimed" land. It is in the middle of the shallow Stanahan River.

Map Scale

What you have been looking at during your journey from the moon or your descent in an airplane are all the features that are included on the maps of your neighborhood that you can buy or look at in your local library. Cities, highways, street patterns, shopping centers, parks, schools, factories, your house, and your yard will all be on a map. In fact, they will probably be on several different maps.

If there are lots of buildings, streets, and parks on the map, and they are shown very small, then the map is a "small-scale" map. Small-scale maps usually show quite a large area. If the map you are looking at shows only a part of your neighborhood, but the buildings are shown quite large, and the streets are quite wide, then you have a "large-scale" map.

So, the view of the earth from the moon or from the airplane really high above the earth is small-scale. The view of your neighborhood from an airplane coming in to land or of the bird flying over your house is a large-scale view.

It is possible to make a map of your area by going into it and surveying all the objects on the ground. That usually involves complicated and expensive equipment that can measure very accurately. But you can do it yourself using some simple techniques. The size of buildings, the length of roads, the area of parkland, and the distances between landmarks can all be measured, and these measurements can be drawn into a map.

However, organizations and companies that take aerial photographs from aircraft with special cameras are more likely to have produced the type of maps that show your local area. All the measurements needed for the map can be taken from the aerial photographs instead of on the ground.

There is a strong link between what the bird sees or what the camera taking a picture from an airplane records and the map that shows what your neighborhood looks like. The "bird's-eye-view" and the photograph are views from straight above looking straight down. The map is made from the photograph but is better in many ways for showing things that you cannot see on the photograph. Such things include street names and types of buildings. But both the aerial photograph and the map are great ways of getting an informative view of your local area.

Your Schoolroom from Above

Imagine you are producing a simple map of your schoolroom. If you are standing at the front of the room where your teacher normally stands, you have a reasonable view over the room, but you cannot see everything. A drawing of what you see would not provide as much information as a map.

You can probably see all the desks and the other furniture in the room. Though there might be some bookshelves, for example, on the wall behind you. Also, your view of the desks in front of you is an *oblique* view. You can see the top and the fronts of the desks only, and the chairs are hidden behind the desks from your viewpoint.

If you are preparing a map, you need to imagine yourself, instead, looking straight down at all the desks and chairs, your teacher's table, and the other pieces of furniture that are in the room.

The map will be a large-scale map. It will cover a small area–just the schoolroom–and even small features, like a wastebasket and a computer, can be shown on it. You will be able to put your own desk on the map as a separate and identifiable object.

To produce this map, you must measure the sizes of these features and the distance from one feature to another. These measurements can be scaled and *plotted* onto a piece of paper or on a computer screen. You may decide that a distance of 1 centimeter on the map will represent a distance of 1 meter (100 centimeters) in the real world. The scale of this map is written as 1:100 and described as "one to one hundred" or "one over one hundred." This means that one unit of measurement on the map is equivalent to 100 units of measurement in the real world.

Every feature that is 1 meter long in your schoolroom, for example, the teacher's desk, will be drawn 1 centimeter long on the map. If your desk is $\frac{1}{2}$ meter (50 centimeters) long and $\frac{1}{2}$ meter wide, it will be drawn on the map as a square measuring $\frac{1}{2}$ centimeter long by $\frac{1}{2}$ centimeter wide.

The first measurements to make are the lengths of the walls of the schoolroom, since everything else will be mapped inside the shape of the room. If the room is a regular shape with straight walls, you can plot the measurements easily on a sheet of graph paper or squared paper. Most of the furniture in the schoolroom–the desks, tables, and bookshelves–will also be rectangular and easy to measure and plot.

See Also: *Making Symbols* **1**: *16–17*

► The map of the class-room is a "straight down" view. It allows you to see all the tables and monitors, along with the location of features hidden from the photograph—like the wastebaskets, the blackboard, and the doors.

▼ The classroom viewed not directly from above, but from an "oblique" viewpoint. You cannot see all the objects in the classroom from this angle.

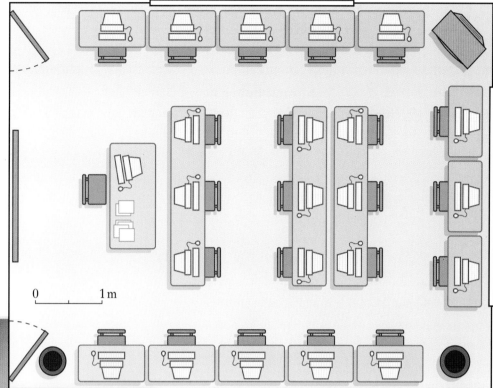

0   1 m

Personal Design

So far your map has some lines drawn on it out-lining the shape of the room and showing where the furniture is. You may want to add some extra information and add your own design features to make it appear more attractive and informative. It is possible to do this with a map.

You could show the position of your desk, for example, by drawing it in a different color from everybody else's desk. You could add the teacher's name to the table at the front of the schoolroom. You could describe which blocks on the map are chairs and which block is the television.

As long as the map does not become too crowded or difficult to read, you can add your own ideas. Your map is based on measurements and is there-fore accurate. It is your personal design preferences that will affect its overall appearance. If your teacher assigns your class this task, giving the same instructions to everyone, each person will probably produce a slightly different map.

Photographs and Maps

A major difference between a photograph of an object and a drawing of the same object is that the photograph shows all the detail, but the drawing highlights the aspects that the artist thinks are important. In the same way maps, which are drawings, are selective pictures of the world.

If you draw the view of your classroom from above, you can highlight the edges of objects, like tables or chairs, using lines (see page 10). But you can also produce a drawing that emphasizes certain objects by coloring in areas. In a similar way aerial photographs of a landscape are different from maps of the same area because the mapmaker chooses what to emphasize. The maps may concentrate on features in the landscape such as lines (like roads or fences) or areas (like lakes or forests).

Many maps use both lines and shaded or colored areas, along with symbols at certain points, like railroad crossings or mountain summits. Together they create a representation of the real world that is a picture, not a photograph.

The labels on the photographs below show the advantages of a photograph in giving information. The labels on the maps indicate examples of things that maps can show better than photographs.

If you look at the aerial photograph of the city, you can see a very detailed image of a complicated landscape, almost completely man-made. There are many objects in the photograph that you might expect to see represented on a map of the same area: buildings, roads, and railroads. The mapmaker has taken measurements from the photograph and created the map you can see alongside. The types of buildings, here the hotel and post office, are shown in words, and the pattern of the roads is much clearer. The photograph cannot show this sort of information, but mapmakers can use other sources to find out about these extra facts.

The aerial photograph of the agricultural area on page 13 shows the dividing up of the landscape into

▼ Urban landscape

Urban vegetation

Heights of some buildings

Full detail of alleys and buildings

Full extent of station

Road name

Editing Visual Information

Different types of landscape produce different scenes in aerial photographs. Many features on the photographs are ignored or modified when a map of the area is drawn. The map can highlight features and simplify complex photographs.

Mapping of features hidden underground

Name of feature

Crown Plaza

Post office here

Car parking public or private

Hotel

P

P

I 395

Type of building

SEE ALSO: MEASURING FROM PHOTOGRAPHS **2:** 22–25; VISUALIZATION **8:** 32–33

fields (areas) using fences and hedges (lines). The mapmaker has taken measurements from the photograph of the length and direction of the field boundaries and plotted them on a map.

There has been a loss of some information from the photograph to the map, such as the variation in the crop pattern within the fields. You cannot see on the map that one of the bottom fields has been plowed. The mapmaker has made the unusual decision to show the area of the trees in a light green color. Unless you check the area symbols for the map, you would never guess that those areas were woods, something you can easily see in the photograph. This is an example of poor design by the mapmaker.

But the map does make clear some features that are difficult to pick out from the photograph. For example, some of the field boundaries are difficult to trace completely on the photograph, but they have all been included on the map. The map also leaves out information that is not necessary, such as the shadows of trees.

Advantages and Disadvantages

Photographs show the world at the time they were taken, perhaps when it was snowing or cloudy. Maps try to ignore this and show a more general picture. Photographs can show only what is visible to the camera. Maps can add other information, including interpretations by the mapmaker.

In some cases it is very difficult to make a map of an area if the photograph does not show objects that can be easily converted into lines and areas that a mapmaker can draw. The infrared photograph of the tidal zone (below) shows all the variation in surface characteristics—sand, grasses, salt meadows, and marsh. It is a difficult scene to map.

The mapmaker has decided to show the location of the thick seaweed by using an area symbol. He has also highlighted deep channels of water, but has ignored all the inland detail in the top right area of the photograph. These decisions suggest that the map is to be used by sailors looking for safe routes. Different people need different kinds of maps.

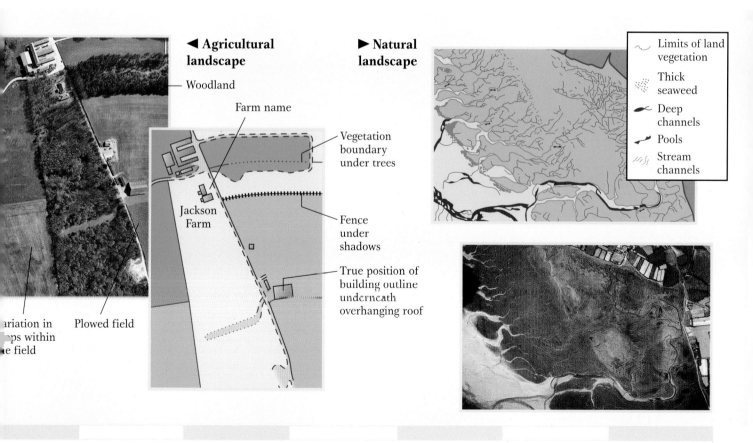

◀ **Agricultural landscape**

— Woodland

Farm name

Jackson Farm

Vegetation boundary under trees

Fence under shadows

True position of building outline underneath overhanging roof

...ariation in ...ps within ...e field

Plowed field

▶ **Natural landscape**

∿ Limits of land vegetation

Thick seaweed

Deep channels

Pools

Stream channels

Generalization

As we have seen, even though they may cover the same area, an aerial photograph and a map are different in appearance and show different things. The most obvious difference is that the aerial photograph shows *all* the complicated detail of a landscape, while the map tries to show only important features and leaves out the minor elements. The smaller the scale of the map, the more essential it is to ensure that the way features are highlighted is not confusing.

The technique of making sure that the map is simplified as the scale gets smaller is called *generalization*. In fact, generalization is the name for several different things that a mapmaker can do when making a map. First, leaving out the minor elements on a map drawn from aerial photographs is one generalization method. A map of a countryside area may leave out many minor roads and tracks and show only the more important connecting highways.

The second form of generalization is to emphasize some features, making them more obvious on the map than they are in the real world. So, we may make the highways that we have included deliberately thicker so that they can be seen clearly. Some highways may be drawn much wider than the rivers on the same map. In the real world it may be the rivers that are wider.

Generalization also simplifies the intricate parts of the real world so that the map is not as complex

▼ **Medium Scale** As the scale increases, more detail is shown. More cities are located and named, and the more important highways and rivers are also included.

▲ **Small Scale** This map of the eastern U.S. shows very little detail. The only features are the coastline, the location of big cities, and the states.

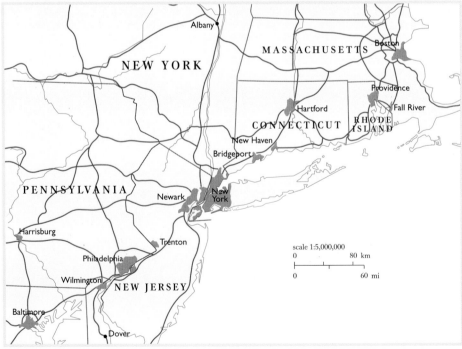

SEE ALSO: *CHOOSING AND DESCRIBING MAP SCALE* **2**: *32–33*; *URBAN TRANSPORTATION MAPS* **7**: *34–35*

as nature. For example, the rivers on the maps here actually have many more bends and curves than shown. The mapmaker has deliberately smoothed the line to give only an impression of the river, rather than a true-to-life representation.

Generalization makes big changes in what we see in the real world. The city area on the map below is, in fact, a combination of many individual buildings along with their surrounding areas of gardens, parks, parking lots, open spaces, and pedestrian zones. Generalization has "characterized" the area and indicates that this part of the map is of an urban type of landscape. The person reading the map is expected to understand the nature of the real world in these areas by interpreting the map.

Topographic and Thematic Maps

Each of the maps on pages 14 and 15 is a topographic map. They are maps that show the landscape and what is on it. They are usually made by official organizations, like government national mapping agencies. The largest-scale topographic maps are created using large-scale aerial photographs, and the

features they show tend to be the kind of features found on these photographs—roads, buildings, and rivers. The large-scale maps are then generalized in order to create smaller-scale maps.

The effect of generalization becomes more and more important as the scale becomes smaller. If you are showing the whole country on one map, a lot of care is needed to make sure that the representation of the real world is not misleading as you select some features and ignore others, emphasize some of them and simplify others.

Generalization is also part of the design of other kinds of maps that are not topographic. A map that is *thematic*, for example, a map providing information about the weather or history or a road map, also has to be generalized. The map showing the weather is unlikely to include the location of schools or railroads. Through generalization these features are left out, and only relevant information, such as the mountain ranges and the shoreline, are selected.

A map showing a historical event like a battle will emphasize certain features, such as the vegetation at a battle site. Thick woodland may have provided cover for soldiers. It will emphasize fortifications, showing trenches or gun emplacements. It may try to show the movements of troops using arrows. But generalization will simplify the complex features of buildings if they were not part of the historical events.

Road maps are normally very generalized, with perhaps only the positions of towns and the coastline retained along with the pattern and types of the roads themselves.

◄ **Large Scale** This map of New York City has been generalized the least. It is a larger-scale map and shows the outline of the built-up area. There is also room on the map to highlight locations such as the Statue of Liberty and some airports.

Making Symbols

If a map has to emphasize features and perhaps show them as more prominent on the map than they are to scale in the real world, then symbols are used for those features. In fact, all maps consist of symbols. Maps are diagrams of the physical world. Or they are thematic diagrams designed to present a specific kind of information about an area: the number and location of bears in the U.S., for example. Maps are all "symbolic"–they represent something: the physical world or some information about the world.

Cartographers (mapmakers) can use their imaginations and their design skills to create a range of pictures or designs. There are many different kinds of maps, and the symbols that are used on them vary greatly. However, there are four main types of symbols that can be used on a map.

The first type are "point" symbols used to stand for features that exist at exact locations in the real world, like a mountain peak, a campsite, or a bus stop. For small-scale maps even towns and cities could be shown by point symbols because they are such small features compared to the large area that a very small-scale map covers.

The point symbols can be simple geometrical shapes, such as dots, small circles, or squares, or they can be more like little pictures, for example, of a mountain, a tent, or a bus. Because the symbols represent complex features in the real world, you could design them as very intricate drawings. But that would be a mistake because symbols on a map should not stand out too much, and the map reader should not have to spend a long time trying to figure them out.

The second type of symbol on a map is the "line" symbol. Line symbols are used to represent rivers and coastlines–physical features–but they can also represent boundaries such as state lines or country frontiers. Again, it is possible to vary the

appearance of these symbols. Lines can be solid or dotted. They can also be drawn in different thicknesses. The major highway in the illustrations on these pages has one thick blue line and two more black lines on either side.

"Area" symbols are used on maps to show features like marshes, lakes, and city zones. The most common area symbols are just one color, such as a blue symbol for the sea and yellow for sand. Some

✆	Telephone	⌂	Caravan site
♜	Castle	▯	Lighthouse
⋔	TV or radio mast	═══	Secondary road
✖	Windmill	━━━	Main road
✝	Church	▬▬▬	Highway
✿	Ancient site	– · – · –	District boundary
Ⓟ	Car park	– – – –	Footpath
		────	Railway line

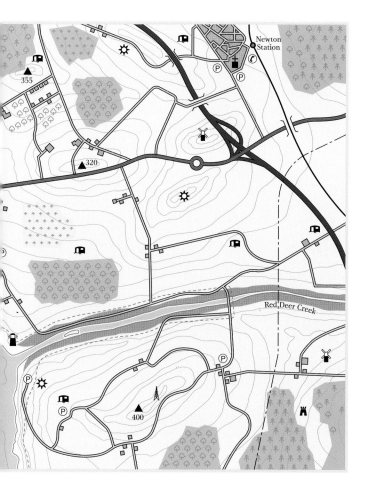

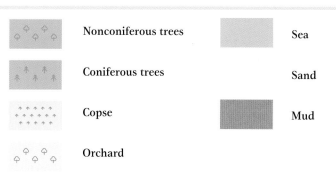

	Nonconiferous trees		Sea
	Coniferous trees		Sand
	Copse		Mud
	Orchard		

of them include a little more decoration, like the symbols for trees used here that have a simple picture of the tree type drawn on them. Patterns are also used within the area symbols for copse and orchard.

The final type of symbol used on maps is one that we are familiar with from other methods of giving information. Maps use text–written letters and numbers–a great deal.

The map on the left tells us that a particular river is called "Red Deer Creek." We are told the name of the rail station We learn that the hill in the top left corner is 355 feet high. The design of text symbols has to be done with care. Simple, easy-to-read letters and numbers should be used on maps.

Color, Shape, and Size

One of the most obvious variations on a map is color. Different colors can be made to represent a range of different features–often blue for water features, green for vegetation features, and brown for landscape features.

There are no strict rules for applying color to maps, but over the years many maps have used regular color designs like these.

Point symbols have different shapes, such as the circular "ancient site" symbol and the triangular height indicators on the illustrations here.

Another variation can be in size. It is useful when symbols are being designed to represent features in the real world that are similar but of different sizes. For example, the circle representing a small village may the same shape and color as the symbol representing a large city, but would be smaller on the map.

Every time we make a map, we have to design some symbols to use. And we must remember to let the person who is reading the map know what the symbols mean. Every map, therefore, should have a *legend* (sometimes called a *key*) that shows all the symbols and tells the map reader what they represent.

◄ This map is designed with point and line symbols. They can represent a wide range of features in the landscape. It does not give as much information as the map of the same area above; but because it shows less, it is easier to read.

▲ This map has more features represented by symbols. Area symbols have been added along with some text. As long as a map has a "key" or "legend" to explain the meaning of the symbols, the mapmaker is free to design an attractive map.

Map Materials through History

The maps that you are familiar with from your school atlas or from watching the weather forecast on the TV look very different than some of the maps in this book, particularly the older ones. The reason for this is that the methods and materials used to produce maps have changed so much since the first ones were made thousands of years ago.

Maps still rely on measurements of the world, as they always have done, but the way in which these measurements are presented has changed. Usually the change has been gradual.

For example, the material people preferred to draw maps on changed from papyrus (used for maps from early Egyptian times to about 300 A.D.) to parchment (used from Roman times to the Middle Ages) over a period of centuries.

Sometimes the improvement has been more sudden. The introduction of specialized printing techniques in the early 1800s changed the production of maps much more quickly.

Some historians think that cartography started tens of thousands of years ago. There are sketches and carvings on bare rock that have been dated back to 30,000 B.C., and some of them have been interpreted as the earliest maps. But it is difficult to know when true cartography started. The earliest diagrams that definitely represent real features like paths, streams, and trees can be dated to about 3000 B.C. These maps appeared as patterns chiseled into hard rock faces.

The materials used for maps changed as societies throughout the world developed. Maps from the Near East (in present-day Iran and Iraq) from about 1500 B.C. were carved onto wet clay tablets that were then dried in the sun. Many of them have been preserved and can be found in museums.

▲ Egyptian agricultural scenes on papyrus, from 1100 B.C. The lines are amazingly sharp after all that time.

Flexibility

Papyrus, invented in Egypt, was not so long lasting. It was the material for many of the maps used by soldiers and administrators and placed in the tombs of kings. These maps used colored ink drawn onto sheets and rolls of papyrus. Papyrus is made from a type of reed grown in marshy areas. The great advantage of papyrus, apart from greater clarity and therefore greater accuracy of any markings, was lightness and flexibility.

From as early as 200 B.C. maps were drawn on a different kind of material made of cleaned, stretched animal skins. It was called parchment. (A fine, delicate kind of parchment, made of the best skins of calves and young goats, was called vellum.) Parchment was still being used for books (often produced in monasteries) many centuries later, in the Middle Ages.

Paper was invented in China and was not introduced to the rest of the world until 610 A.D. It gradually became the most popular material to draw maps on, and of course, it is still the most common

SEE ALSO: THE EARLIEST MAPS **1**: 20–21; URBAN TRANSPORTATION MAPS **7**: 34–35

method of producing *hard-copy*, printed maps. Paper is the material that most modern printing uses. Instead of being hand drawn, maps can be produced once and then be reproduced in thousands of copies, all exactly the same.

From the 1800s to the present day map printing has developed significantly. The most important technique is called *lithography*. It uses metal printing plates and large printing presses that can produce thousands of copies per hour on large sheets of paper.

Today, most maps are drawn on computer screens. These maps are different from conventional printed maps because they disappear when the computer is switched off! They are called *soft-copy* or temporary maps. Using up-to-date computer programs, it is possible to draw high-quality maps without having to sketch the map in freehand.

Almost anyone can use computer software to create good maps, and it is then possible to print out what is produced. You do not need expensive printing presses to produce a map today.

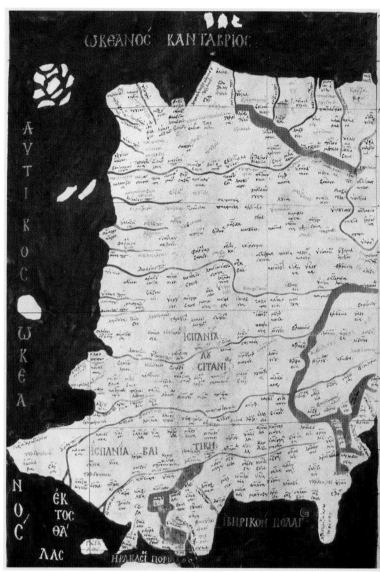

▲ An illuminated manuscript on vellum of Ptolemy's map of Spain and Portugal, produced in the 15th century. The gold lettering is real gold leaf.

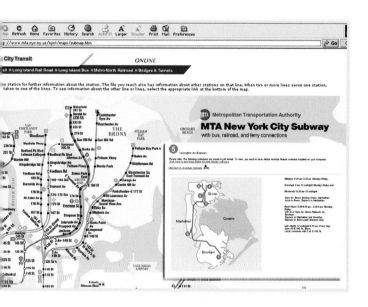

▲ Most maps today are produced on computer screens, like this subway map delivered using the World Wide Web. The Internet makes looking for maps much easier than it was when only books could be consulted.

Some map users rely on computer-drawn maps in their everyday life. For example, the airplane pilot, the ambulance driver, and the geologist can all use computer maps in their vehicle, on their desktop, or on their cell phone. The maps still contain the point, line, area, and text symbols that all maps have contained for thousands of years. But they have been drawn by computer and are presented on screens that would astonish our ancestors.

The Earliest Maps

Since the earliest maps were created thousands of years ago, they have continued to help people make sense of their surroundings. The first maps did include information about things like rivers and forests, like a modern map. But they also must have helped people feel as if they understood the world a little better. The earliest people must have found the world a frightening place, full of things they could not explain. Anything that helped make sense of it–like a map–was welcome.

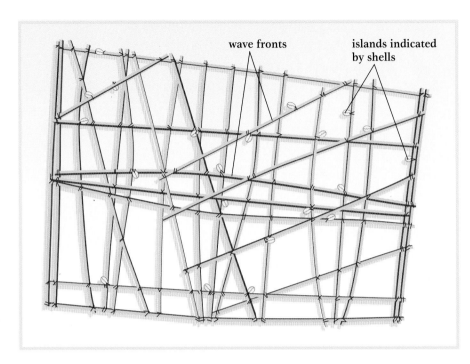

wave fronts

islands indicated by shells

▲ This map of ocean currents and islands was made out of reeds. It comes from the South Pacific and helped people traveling in dugout canoes and out-riggers to find their way from island to island.

Maps can be made of small areas such as your own local region or the largest possible area, the universe. They can help us communicate our thoughts and ideas about places to other people. Sometimes maps can tell a story, for example, "Here is a route map showing where we went." They can store facts: "You can check on the map that the mountain ahead of us is the highest one in the area." Or they can explain relationships between things: "Our town expanded because it is sited at a good place where two rivers meet, as shown on the map."

Maps have been produced for longer than languages or numbers have been written down, so they are one of the oldest forms of human communication. It seems that most of our ancestors living thousands of years ago were able to create maps. Mapping is a natural human skill–certainly no other animals can do it! (Though some creatures seem to have extremely accurate "mental maps" of the world, like birds that migrate over thousands of miles.)

The earliest people had certain advantages that gave them this skill. They were highly mobile and moved around their environment easily, mainly to hunt and gather food. They also had a sense of

direction that helped them remember the best places to find food and how to return to them. So they had a good knowledge of the landscape and the features on it.

Human beings have good eyesight, letting them see a large part of the landscape in one view, which helps when it comes to mapmaking. Finally, it is clear from looking at prehistoric art that our ancestors were able to draw well.

Three Early Types of Map

What kinds of maps did these ancient peoples produce? They can be divided into three types. First, there were maps of the area in which they lived. These maps were local and were drawn from observing the features in the physical world, like forests, rivers, and mountains. They were usually based on the walking distances that tribes recorded. It might take, for example, half a day to reach a

SEE ALSO: *MAP MATERIALS THROUGH HISTORY* **1:** *18–19; EXPLORATION AND MAPMAKING* **5:** *6–7*

spring used as a water source. A hunting ground might actually be the same distance away, but it might take two day's hike across mountains to reach it. The map would represent the time measurement rather than the distance measurement.

Some early Neolithic diagrams (from 5000 B.C.) showed complicated symbols, sometimes people or animals; they also show some *generalization* in their production. Although they depict the local environment, these maps were produced on permanent surfaces like rock faces, so they are unlikely to have been used for navigation. (A navigation map is of limited use if you cannot take it with you on your journey.) Instead, these early maps were probably used for ceremonies and acted as symbols for the tribe. They helped give a feeling of belonging, of being "at home."

The second type of map was of the sky—the stars, planets, and their changing patterns. Many prehistoric patterns found scratched on stone surfaces represent the arrangement of stars, the *constellations*. They are not true maps because they have no proper scale, but they do accurately show the relationships between objects in the night sky.

The final type of map was not drawn as a result of observation. It was based on stories and myths, especially about how the earth was created.

These *cosmological* maps showed the whole earth (not just a small part of it) and also portrayed features like the underworld, heaven, and the places where other mythical creatures might live. They are described in the next section.

▲ Ancient petroglyphs (stone carvings) in Nootka on the Canadian coast. No one knows if they are maps or boundary markers.

◄ This is a local map drawn on a cave wall in the Camonica Valley of northern Italy. It shows a pattern of fields, tracks, and rivers, and is estimated to date from the Bronze Age, around 1500 B.C.

Trying to Explain the Universe with Maps

Early peoples were concerned with the relationship between the earth and the rest of the universe. That was because they felt that their day-to-day life depended on the continuous working of nature in patterns that had been established by gods or processes of creation. If the world could be positioned on a map that showed those processes, perhaps it would be easier to avoid disaster, or at least to understand why it happened.

People thought that interruptions to day-to-day life like thunderstorms, earthquakes, *eclipses*, planetary movements, and plagues needed to be explained, and order needed to be restored. Rituals such as sacrifices and worship were intended to reestablish order. The real world was not just made up of trees and rivers and animals. It included the relationship between the earth (and humankind which lived on it) and the rest of the universe.

Many myths grew up about the creation of the world, and they had a significant effect on the way different peoples viewed the world. The creation stories explained how the land, sea, and sky were created and how human beings came into existence. Creation stories varied, and any maps based on them also varied. These mythological stories that explained the creation and place of the earth existed in all cultures.

Some Chinese and Japanese accounts suggested the universe was something like an egg–the yolk representing the earth and the surrounding white representing the mysterious "waters" of the heavens.

▶ One of the oldest maps in existence, this Babylonian clay tablet shows the whole of the earth as a disk surrounded by ocean and with some heavenly bodies around the outer ring. It is a map based on ancient philosophy, carved in the 7th century B.C.

The mythical story of Pan-ku, the Chinese primeval man, is a development of the egg legend. Eighteen thousand years after being born from the original cosmic egg, Pan-ku died.

His head formed the sun and moon. His blood became the water on the earth's surface. His sweat formed the rain. His hair created the forests, and his breath produced the winds. His voice was thunder. And the fleas that lived on his body? They became the ancestors of human beings!

SEE ALSO: *MAPPING BEFORE SCIENTIFIC MEASUREMENT* **2:** 6–7

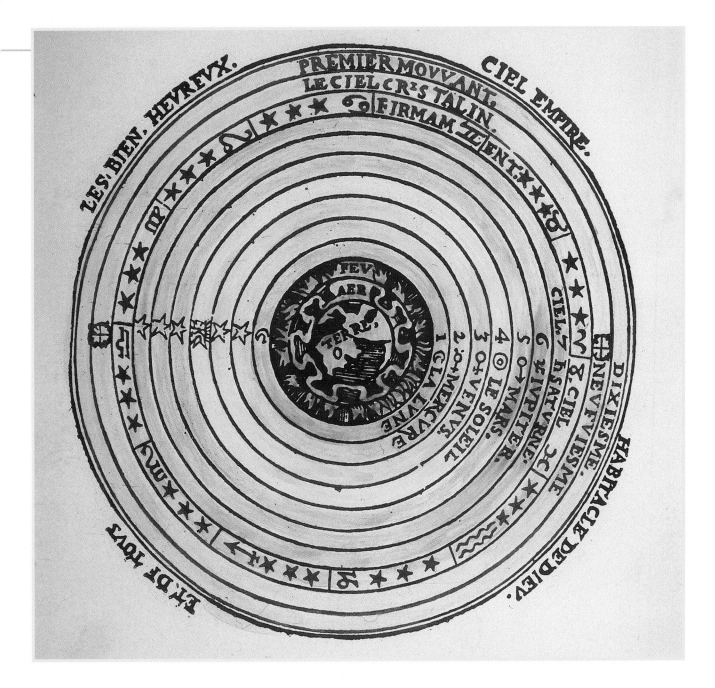

Layers and Shapes

As human societies developed, they began to consider the arrangement of the features of the world. An early idea was of "layers" of physical features. The Sumerian peoples, creators of one of the earliest civilizations, lived about 5,000 years ago where the Tigris and Euphrates Rivers meet (now in southern Iraq). They thought that the earth had a layer underneath, a vast underground reservoir called Abzu, which fed the rivers and kept them flowing even when no rain fell.

Ancient Egyptians thought that the sky was a layer above the earth supported on four giant pillars.

▲ This 16th-century diagram shows the ancient plan of the universe as proposed by Greek astronomers. The earth is at the center, with the planets orbiting around it—La Lune (the moon), Mercure (Mercury), Venus, Le Soleil (the sun), etc. It was an interpetation of what could really be seen in the sky, not a mythical story.

Some other civilizations imagined circles and spheres instead of flat layers. Both Hindu philosophy in India and the much later Roman civilization thought of the universe as a series of spheres fitted inside each other. Early Judaism shared a similar view of the sky as a solid spherical dome with window holes through which rain fell.

There were other myths about the shape of the world itself. Chinese philosophy of the Han dynasty up to the second century B.C. pictured it as a square, and some Indian philosophers thought of the earth as a maze. The Babylonians pictured the earth as a hollow mountain floating in a sea.

All the maps drawn from these stories and beliefs were simple diagrams that represented the whole of the universe and the earth, with the earth normally the biggest part. In order to make maps based on these views more convincing, some of the real objects in the world were included, like the sea and the mountain ranges.

Observations and Calculations

As civilizations developed, maps came to rely less and less on the imagination and more and more on what people could see with their own eyes. At the same time as the priests and philosophers were thinking about the structure of the universe in a theoretical and philosophical way, some people were making practical observations of the movement of stars and planets. The pattern of stars was recognized as being permanent, although the movement of the planets

▲ Ancient Indian observatories still stand today in cities such as Jaipur, Delhi, and Varanasi. Astronomers from India had well-developed ideas about the nature of the universe. The buildings were designed to line up with heavenly bodies so that calculations could be made about the movement of the stars.

was less constant. The signs of the *Zodiac* in the sky and the regular pattern of the seasons suggested a natural order in the universe.

Some Important Astronomers

This new science influenced the development from about 500 B.C. of Greek cartography. The Greeks assumed the planets moved around the perfectly spherical earth and that these orbits were also perfectly circular and predictable.

Such observations continued through the centuries. Scientific thought in Western societies became more mature in the late Middle Ages with, first, the observations of the Polish astronomer Copernicus (1473–1543). Other important scientists of that time were the German Johannes Kepler (1571–1630) and Galileo

SEE ALSO: *FINDING YOUR WAY BY THE STARS* **4:** *6–7*

(1564–1642), who lived in Florence and Padua in Italy.

These practical astronomers based their views of the universe on their observations of the sky and mathematical calculations. They correctly worked out a number of facts that confirmed the true place of the earth within the universe.

Copernicus was the first to suggest that the earth orbits around the sun, rather than the other way around. Kepler figured out that the orbits of the planets are in fact *elliptical*, rather than circular. And Galileo made important discoveries about the moons that orbit other planets in predictable ways.

Mankind's search for order has been long, and it is still going on. Maps showing the earth's position in the cosmos are constantly being revised as we reach out with ever more powerful telescopes and with space probes to explore more of the universe. Maps showing the nature of the earth itself, however, now have a fixed and accepted framework within which features can be properly positioned, recorded, and presented.

Today maps are made using measurements and photographs of the world, and it is only some of the remaining aboriginal tribes who view the earth and its place in the universe in the same way as our ancestors did thousands of years ago.

▼ An 18th-century Buddhist, Tibetan map of the world. Mount Sumeru, the center of the universe, is in the inner circle. It is surrounded by the four continents and their islands in the cosmic ocean. This map was not produced though observation of the physical world.

▼ The world as seen by the Powhatans, American Indians whose Algonquin tribe took Captain John Smith prisoner in Virginia in 1607. They put the home of stranger John Smith at the edge of the world. Though originally drawn without ink, it is still a map.

Maps of Ancient Civilizations

In the ancient world aspects of learning and technology that would be important for mapmaking developed at different rates in different societies. Paper and a grid system for positioning things on it would come from the East. The idea of map projections would come from the West.

In areas of Europe and around the Mediterranean important and well-developed civilizations grew up from about 2500 B.C. On the banks of the Nile River the ancient Egyptian society flourished and was able to undertake extraordinary feats of construction. The famous Great Pyramids at Giza, near Cairo, were built from 2700 B.C. to 1000 B.C. Such work required accurate measurements.

In addition, the Egyptians needed to measure land boundaries and find out who owned each piece of land so that fields and farms could be marked out. Every year the annual flood of the Nile River washed away the boundary markers, so the legal owners needed to be recorded in some way. Both construction and land recording needed well-trained surveyors and mapmakers to measure positions on the ground and keep registers in the form of maps.

Most of these maps crumbled to dust a long time ago because they were produced on papyrus (the ancient Egyptian form of paper), which was very fragile. A few have been preserved, mostly in ancient tombs, and have been dug up by archaeologists.

Other practical activities called on the services of mapmakers in ancient Egypt. Much of the wealth of the kingdoms along the Nile came from gold mines in the hills bordering the Red Sea to the east. They were important to the Egyptian kings, and plans of their gold mines have been discovered in some of their tombs. Other more personal maps were also placed within the graves underneath pyramids. Maps have been found showing the route to the "afterlife" to be used by the spirits of the dead kings. They form part of the *Books of the Dead*, which were meant to be guides to the "afterlife."

Practical Use and Theory Combine

The Egyptians, over a period of many hundreds of years, also developed techniques of astronomical observation, but they seemed less interested than some other societies in the place of the earth in the universe. They did have their own particular stories of the creation of the sea, land, and sky; but they were not often shown in the form of maps. Pictures

▲ An engraving of the goddess Urania (Greek goddess of astronomy, at right) inspiring Ptolemy in his work. He is using a sextant to find the position of the stars.

SEE ALSO: *INFORMATION FROM TRAVELERS* **2:** *8–9;* *HOW TO MAKE MEASUREMENTS FOR MAPS* **2:** *12–17*

of mapmakers have survived on tomb walls and in long-buried temples. In these illustrations they are preparing maps for everyday tasks like construction, reclaiming land from the desert and the sea, boundary and ownership surveys, and military expeditions.

Egyptian influence over the eastern Mediterranean region was enormous for a very long period. It was not until Alexander the Great invaded in 332 B.C. that Egypt started to absorb the ideas of other

▲ An ancient map of the Red Sea hills of Egypt showing roads between the Nile River and the Red Sea as well as the important gold-mining settlements. This papyrus map dates from about 1250 B.C.

civilizations. By that time Greek philosophers had developed theories about the shape of the earth and the outlines of the land and sea. Many of the Greeks believed that nature was perfect and that the precise form of the earth therefore had to be the perfect shape, a sphere. That seemed to be confirmed by

▼ A reconstruction of a map by Ptolemy (bottom) showing most of Europe and large parts of Africa and Asia. The Greeks thought that the Indian Ocean (Oceanus Indicus) was surrounded by land. When the Americas were discovered 1,400 years after Ptolemy, his projection method was used to map them (below).

looking at the curved shadow of the earth on the moon during an eclipse.

The importance of observations and measurement became more and more clear to the Greeks during the period from 500 B.C. to the time of Ptolemy, the most famous Greek geographer. Ptolemy, who lived from 90 to 168 A.D., not only made maps, he also wrote books on how to make maps and prepared lists of information (most importantly, the locations of towns in the ancient world) that could be used in mapmaking.

He was one of the first cartographers to find out how to show the sphere on a flat piece of paper, using *map projections*. The map on this page shows his projection and the kind of information that he

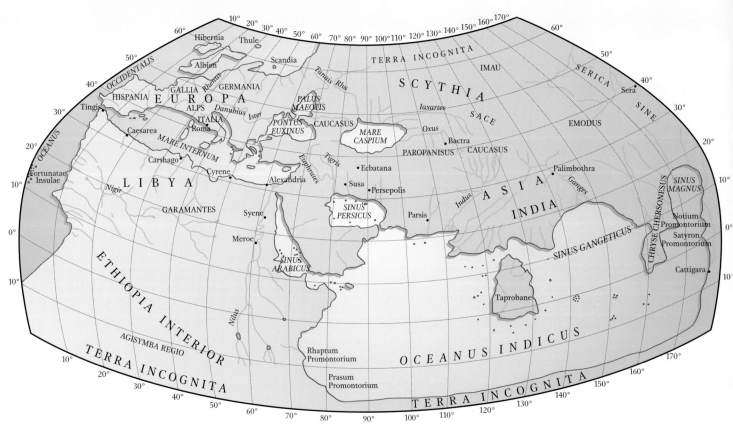

SEE ALSO: EXPLORATION AND MAPMAKING **5:** 6–7; CHINESE AND JAPANESE URBAN PLANS **7:** 10–11

▲ This faded map of a palace complex is from a Korean atlas, but the writing in the atlas is all Chinese. The "Yojido" atlas was produced in the 1760s.

was able to put on his maps. He suggested ways of dividing up the world so that maps of countries and smaller regions could be produced.

The Greek cartographers did not create large numbers of maps to be used for practical tasks, as the Egyptians did. They wanted to record the whole world, and their maps that have survived and the maps that are copies derived from their writings show the extent of Western geographical knowledge at the beginning of the first millennium.

Eastern Civilizations

The first Chinese dynasties (organized societies with a series of kings) developed in about 2200 B.C., and like other early civilizations, they had their own philosophical view of the world. Stories about the creation of the universe and the world were important in early Chinese mapping, but a more scientific approach followed. Tools for measurement and for preparing maps in China became advanced long before they did in the Western civilizations

around the Mediterranean. Paper had replaced wooden strips for writing on by the 4th century B.C., long before its use in the West.

The early astronomer Chang Heng introduced the idea of a map based on a grid system that allows you to read locations off the map easily. This rectangular system is still used today.

A Chinese engineer, Phei Hsiu, who lived in the third century A.D., wrote instruction books on how to make maps. He also created a list of names (called a *gazetteer*) of important places throughout China and prepared some up-to-date maps covering the whole country. Phei Hsiu used techniques of land surveying and map plotting that were not used in Western civilizations for many centuries.

Instead of being drawn on parchment, early Chinese maps were made using silk. The symbols used on their maps were easy to read, and many of the maps looked very similar to each other in style. That is because China had a strong central government that wanted accurate and uniform maps of the whole country.

The Chinese introduced many of their mapping ideas to other civilizations in Asia, such as the Japanese and Korean societies.

Three-dimensional Mapping

One of the most obvious problems that cartographers face when making a topographic map from an aerial photograph is the fact that the photo is flat (two-dimensional), but we know that the real world has high and low points in it (it is three-dimensional). The map that results from the cartographer's design is also two-dimensional. We need to find a way of showing the hills and valleys of the landscape on a flat piece of paper or on a computer screen, which is also flat.

Cartographers have been tackling this problem for many centuries. Ancient mapmakers realized that maps are representations of the real world looked at straight down from a bird's-eye view. They were aware that the mountains do not look as impressive as they should when you look at them like this. It was important to be able to design a symbol that warned the traveler what he might face: mighty mountain barriers in his way.

For many centuries the only way hills and mountains were shown on maps was by symbols that looked like the landscape viewed by people on the ground. The maps had sketches of the side view of mountains. Some maps had enormous numbers of little sketches of hills scattered across them.

This technique was also used to represent man-made features that stood up above the earth's surface, such as churches or castles. Maps of the Middle Ages showing towns and cities, for example, used small sketches of the city cathedral or the town walls to represent them.

Contour Lines

It was only in the 1800s that mapmakers started to show mountains on maps in the same way as all the other features on maps–looked at straight down

from above. To do this, they needed to invent special symbols that could show the differences in height between the valley and the mountain and show the hill slopes in the real world.

Different symbols have been created for this. The first is the *contour*, a line that joins places on the ground that have the same height. The contour line shows the heights of places above sea level, which is

SEE ALSO: *SHOWING HEIGHT ON FLAT CITY MAPS* **7:** *18–19*

▼ This 1513 map of North Africa shows mountains using sketches that are nowhere near to correct scale.

at a height of 0 feet. All mountaintops are measured, and their height above sea level is shown. If the height of any places on official or standard maps is given, it is always height above sea level.

So, the coastline drawn on a map that shows the edge of the sea has a contour value of 0. A little way inland away from the sea there will be places that are 10 feet (3 m) above sea level, and a contour line can be drawn to join these points together. All the points between this line and the coastline will be between 0 and 10 feet above sea level, but the places on the other side of the line will all be more than 10 feet above sea level.

As you move farther away from the coast, more contours can be drawn; and once you reach the rugged mountains, there will be a complex pattern of lines that shows the height of the landscape at any position on the map.

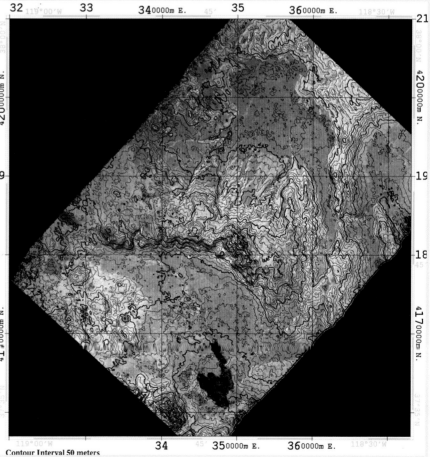

Contour Interval 50 meters

▶ A modern map of the landscape using contours and layer tinting. Contours are lines joining places of equal height above sea level. The pattern of contour lines can represent the shape of hills and valleys. The layer tints (colored areas) also give an impression of the terrain. This map was produced using a computer.

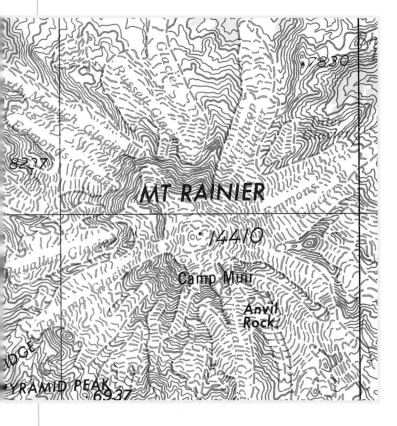

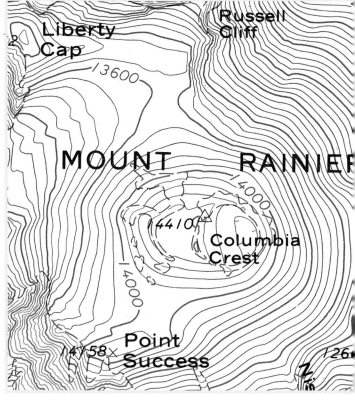

◀ Topographic map of 14,410 ft (4,392 m) Mount Rainier, the volcano that lies 95 miles southeast of Seattle in Washington State. This map, created by the U.S. Geological Survey, is quite small scale. There is no room to put numbers with the contour lines, and they just give an overall impression of mountainous terrain.

▼ On a larger scale contour lines can be labeled with their height every 400 ft (124 m). The contour lines each show a rise of 80 ft (25 m), unlike the contour lines on the map to the left that are shown only every 200 ft (62 m). The map below has room to label Point Success and its height, plus other named high points.

The arrangement of the contour lines can tell the map-reader about the landscape at a glance. Contour lines that are close together indicate a steep slope in that area, but contours that are far apart show little change in height across the area.

So, if you can imagine a mountain standing by itself in the landscape (perhaps a volcano like Mt. Rainier), it will have a contour line going around the bottom joining all the points that are, for example, exactly 1,000 feet (300 m) above sea level. If you were to climb up the mountain another 1,000 feet–measured straight up, not along the ground– you would reach the point where the 2,000-foot contour would be drawn.

If you then walked around the mountain keeping at the same height, you would be following the 2,000-foot contour. Climbing further up the mountain, you would cross the 3,000- and the 4,000-foot contours. These lines each go around the mountain and form smaller and smaller circles, all focused on the summit.

Shading

A second symbol used to show the landscape from above is called a *hachure*. It is a short line that is drawn down the slope (instead of along the slope like a contour). These lines are not used as much as contours, and they are more artistic, trying to sketch out the appearance of the landscape. The hachures are thick lines where the slope is steep and are

thinner where the slope is gentler. They can effectively point out steep cliffs and rock faces.

The artistic sketching of the slopes of the landscape can also be done using shading that tries to show shadows on one side of a hill and brighter areas on the other side. It is difficult to do; but if this hill shading is produced well, it is a very effective way of showing the *relief* (which is the name given to the shape and appearance of the hills and valleys in the landscape). Some computer programs can now help achieve hillshading.

Tinting

Some small-scale maps, like those that show a whole continent, use a sequence of colors to show the changing relief. A common way of doing this is to use the order of colors of the rainbow, producing a gradual change as the landscape rises from sea to

▲ A layer tinted topographical map of the U.S. At this small scale it is easy to see where the highest mountains are—but it is impossible to pick out a specific peak like Mount Rainier.

mountains. The sea is colored blue, then the lowest land close to the coast is shaded in green. As the land rises, the colors on the map change through yellow, orange, red, and finally to purple at the highest peaks. This is called *layer tinting*.

Showing the three-dimensional landscape on maps has been one of the major challenges for cartographers, who have developed improved ways of doing it over many centuries. The designs now use accurate measurements like the height above sea level, but they always demand some artistic ability. There are still problems in showing some three-dimensional features, such as buildings.

Maps of Invisible Things

As we have seen, maps are not photographs. They can include information about a landscape that a photograph cannot supply. But some maps not only give extra information about what can be seen in that landscape, they inform us about things that can never be seen or photographed.

It is possible to make maps of your classroom, your neighborhood, and the world by observing and drawing the features you can see in reality, like your house and your city. But throughout history people have also made maps of things that are invisible, like geological features underground and the orbits of the planets.

Today many maps show features that cannot be seen. A map of an area around an airport could plot the noise levels at different points and at different times. Such a map would be useful when planning where to locate new housing.

In fact, all maps concerned with planning could be regarded as maps of invisible things. They show what could happen in the future rather than what is currently visible in the landscape. The planned new shopping center, the revised road layout, and the altered zoning plan can all be put on a map even though they do not exist at the moment.

As well as depicting the future, maps can show features and things that existed some time in the past. All maps that portray historical events and past landscapes are maps of invisible things. Maps are valuable in our attempts to record and understand our history. We are able to produce maps to explain historical events and to recreate the times in which our ancestors lived. That is done by studying written historical records, examining archaeological evidence, and by redrawing maps actually produced during past times.

Useful Invisible Information

Weather maps look back and into the future. They show some features that are invisible, such as temperature, air pressure, and wind speed, although some things, like rainfall and cloud cover are more obvious. Weather mapping relies on observations taken using instruments like thermometers and barometers in many locations. Forecasting depends on a record of weather patterns over many years.

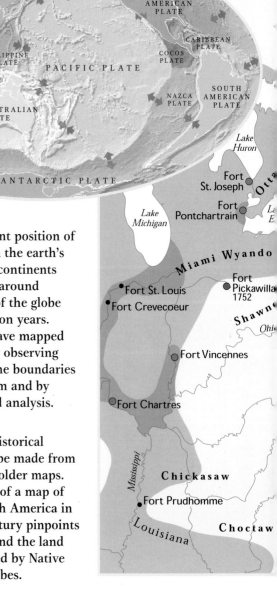

▲ The current position of the plates on the earth's surface; the continents have moved around the surface of the globe for 200 million years. Geologists have mapped the plates by observing features at the boundaries between them and by underground analysis.

▶ Maps of historical periods can be made from records and older maps. This section of a map of eastern North America in the 18th century pinpoints battle sites and the land then occupied by Native American tribes.

SEE ALSO: *MAPPING FEATURES BELOW THE SURFACE* **6:** *16–17; MODERN GEOLOGICAL MAPPING* **8:** *28–29*

Many human activities depend on maps of parts of the earth that are normally invisible to us. Mineral exploration companies, interested in prospecting for valuable metals and fuels, need accurate mapping of the surface features, including the terrain, the vegetation, and water.

In addition, they use sophisticated techniques to map the geological features under the surface. The layers of rock beneath our feet, their type, and their folding or breaking patterns can be found out by detailed analysis of surface and borehole rock samples taken at the site.

Another method is to set off small explosions on the surface and then record the resulting sound echoes from the rocks below ground. Scientists can interpret the echo patterns to find out if, for example, an area is likely to hold oil or coal.

They can also map the continental plates (see picture opposite), vast areas of the world's surface that have drifted apart or pushed into each other over hundreds of millions of years to create mountain ranges and deep trenches.

"Echo-sounding" is also used to map another place invisible to us, the bottom of the sea. Maps that show the depth of the sea are called bathymetric charts. Such *hydrographic charts* are important tools for mariners.

Labels and Statistics

Even standard topographic maps that show landscapes include things that are not visible on the ground. The names of features have to be found from the local residents or from official records before they can be added to the map. Often, such maps also include representations of boundaries between states, counties, and properties. Again, these features are not usually visible on the ground.

Space probes have been sent to travel close to Jupiter, Saturn, and Neptune and to land on Mars and Venus. The information sent back to earth from these probes means that scientists can produce maps of the planet surfaces. Some extra information can also be added to these maps, such as the north and south poles of Mars or the names of large features on the surface of Jupiter.

Back on earth there are many things that can be added to maps. Some things are difficult to calculate by eye, like river flow or traffic density. These aspects of the environment can also be mapped. Statistical measurements can be mapped, like the varying birthrate in different areas or countries, or people's income, or the prevalence of some disease

We do not need to see things to make maps!

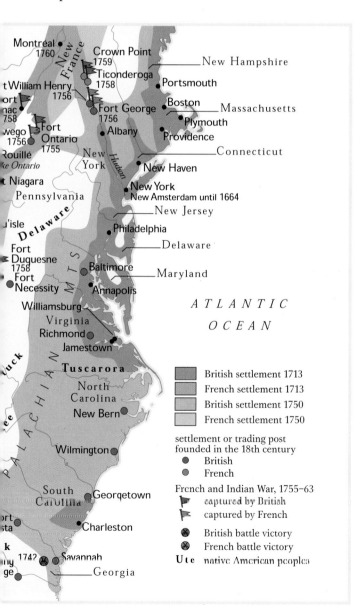

British settlement 1713
French settlement 1713
British settlement 1750
French settlement 1750

settlement or trading post
founded in the 18th century
● British
● French

French and Indian War, 1755–63
⚑ captured by British
⚑ captured by French

⊗ British battle victory
⊗ French battle victory
Ute native American peoples

Your World-view

Every person has his or her own view of the world. The aboriginal tribal chief has a different view from that of the scientific surveyor looking at the same mountains and valleys. So any maps that are made are affected by the opinions, beliefs, and views of the world that the mapmaker has.

As a result, it is difficult to make a map that does not show some bias and influence from the person who makes it. If you were to make a map, the influences that have been with you since you were a young child would affect it. These influences can affect even large-scale maps that are created just from measuring the real world. If you were asked to make a map of your home, for example, you might show your bedroom in great detail, but only show your brother's or your sister's bedroom as an empty outline!

Small-scale mapping is even more influenced by the mapmaker's opinions and beliefs. That is because small-scale maps show a bigger area of the real world, such as a complete country, and can only emphasize some features. You have to ask yourself: Which features are more important than others? What aspects of the country should I

▶ Medieval maps produced in monasteries reflected the views of monks who spent their whole lives in one place, never going beyond their cloisters and local fields. To them Jerusalem (represented by the main towers in the circle in the center of this world map) was the most important place on earth. The monks' world-view came from their reading of the Bible and very little else.

highlight on my map? How should I show this country in relation to its neighbors?

Your own interpretation of the world is an important part of mapmaking. And your interpretation of the world is created and altered by many factors. For example, you may have spent some time on vacation at a seaside tourist destination in an overseas country, like Mexico or Spain, and your view of that country may not include the fact that it has mountains, deserts, and large cities because you did not see them yourself. Your view of the whole world is affected by your experience of traveling in it.

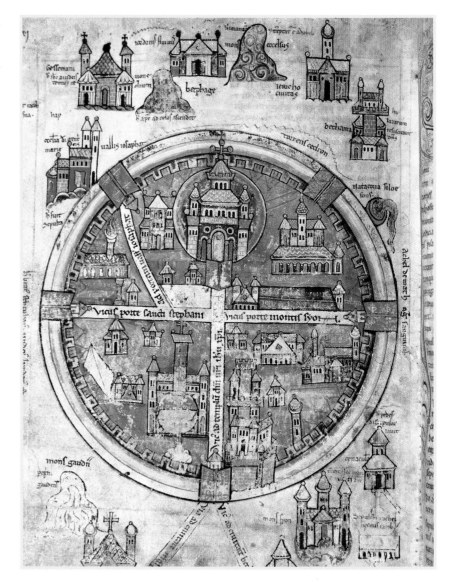

SEE ALSO: *MAPPING BEFORE SCIENTIFIC MEASUREMENT* **2:** *6–7;* MAPPING PEOPLE **6:** *18–19*

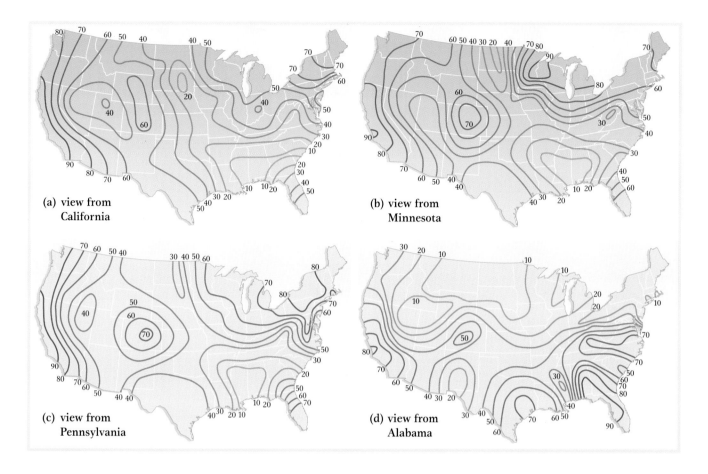

(a) view from California

(b) view from Minnesota

(c) view from Pennsylvania

(d) view from Alabama

A Mental Map

Sometimes you will pick up knowledge of the world from books or the TV. Your view of the world is always being changed by these experiences, and so you have a changing picture of it that you carry in your mind. It can be thought of as a map, a *mental map*, stored in your brain.

You use your mental map, often without thinking, to plan journeys. Choosing the best way to travel from your home to the football stadium is something that you could probably do fairly easily based on your mental map of the roads in your town. Whenever your world-view changes, through your experiences and your education, your mental map is updated.

You also form ideas about places that you have maybe never even visited, like some of the people who were asked where they would most like to live to produce the maps shown above. (The higher the score shown, the more popular the area.)

▲ These maps show the popularity of places to live in the U.S. For someone from Pennsylvania (c) their favorite part of the country is, in fact, California, and they definitely would not like to live in Mississippi or Alabama. But people in Alabama (d) give highest scores to their own state and parts of Florida. Minnesotans (b) like their own state, but also parts of California. It is not difficult to figure out where Californians (a) prefer!

Both making a map and using a map are experiences that can change your world-view. Maps can help you travel; they can help you plan. Maps let us interpret the real world and give us an understanding of how we all live together on this crowded planet. They can bring us together and influence our thinking so that we can see our own place in the world and help make it a better home for everybody.

Sometimes, maps can actually be misleading. They can distort the truth. Maps matter!

Glossary

Words in *italics* have their own entries in the glossary

Aerial photograph (or air photograph) – a photograph looking straight down at the earth, taken from an airplane

Atlas – a collection of maps with a uniform design bound together as a book

Archaeology – the science of interpreting the past by examining remains, usually dug up from underground

Astronomy – the scientific study of celestial bodies (planets and stars) and of the universe as a whole. People who do this are called astronomers

Atmosphere – the thin layer of gases around the earth

Barometer – a scientific instrument used to measure atmospheric pressure, the force of the air pushing down on the earth from above; low pressure usually indicates bad weather

Bathymetric maps or charts – those that show the depths of oceans, seas, and lakes

Bird's-eye view – a straight-down view of the earth

Birthrate – the number of children born in relation to the population of an area or country; often stated as numbers born per 1,000 people in the area

Books of the Dead – Ancient Egyptian texts that were written as guides to the afterlife, containing many of the ideas of Egyptian religion. At first they were inscribed on stone sarcophagi (coffins) but were later written on *papyrus* and put in the mummy case or grave

Cartographer – someone who collects information and produces maps from it; the task of making maps is called cartography

Constellation – a group of stars in the night sky appearing to form a group and normally named with reference to the shape the group takes; for example, the Big Dipper

Contour – an imaginary line connecting places in the landscape that are at equal height above (or below) *sea level*. The distance of contour lines from each other on a map shows how steeply or gradually land rises (*see also* Relief)

Cosmography – the representation of the cosmos (the universe) through maps and diagrams

Cosmology – the study of the cosmos (universe) and how it was created

Eclipse – the total or partial obscuring of one celestial body by another. In a solar eclipse the moon passes in front of the sun, preventing light from reaching the earth. When the earth comes between the sun and the moon (a lunar eclipse), a shadow of the earth is cast onto the moon

Elliptical – oval-shaped, like a distorted (squashed) circle; the orbits of most planets around the sun are elliptical

Equator – an imaginary line running around the earth at equal distance from the North and South *Poles*. It is the line of 0 degrees *latitude*

Gazetteer – a list of names of places, with their location specified; often accompanied by a map

Generalization – the task of simplifying a map, allowing it to portray the most important information even at *small scale*

Globe – the earth; or a map of the earth produced on a sphere

Grid system – a *reference system* that uses a mesh of horizontal and vertical lines over the face of a map to pinpoint the position of places. The mesh of lines often helps show distance of locations east and north from a set position. The *zero point* can be any convenient location and is often the bottom-left corner of the map

Hachure – a short line drawn on a map down the slope of hills and mountains to give an impression of *relief*

Hard-copy map – a map printed on paper that you can carry around with you

Hemisphere – one half of the globe. It is divided into northern and southern hemispheres by the *equator* and into western and eastern hemispheres by the *Prime Meridian*

Hill shading – the sketching of shadows on the sides of hills and mountains on a map that helps the viewer see the map as three-dimensional

Hydrography – the description and study of bodies of water such as seas, lakes, and rivers. Hydrographic charts of oceans and lakes provide navigational information for sailors

Infrared – a part of the spectrum close to red, but detected by the senses as heat, rather than light; infrared radiation is not visible to the eye but can be recorded by some sensors

Key – *see* Legend

Large-scale map – a map that shows a small area with a lot of detail; like a *bird's-eye view* from a low height above the earth

Latitude – a line that joins places of equal angular distance from the center of the earth in a north-south direction. The *equator* is at 0 degrees latitude, the *poles* at 90 degrees latitude north and south

Layer tinting – showing height of mountains and hills on a map using bands of color to define zones where the land is between two height measurements (between 100 and 250 meters above *sea level*, for example)

Legend – a list of all the *symbols* used on a map with an explanation of their meaning

Lithography – a modern printing method, the way in which most printed maps are produced; it allows for quick, cheap, and uniform production of many copies of the same map

Longitude – a line connecting places of equal angular distance from the center of the earth, measured in degrees east or west of the *Prime Meridian*, which is at 0 degrees longitude

Map projection – a method of presenting the curved surface of the earth on a map on a flat piece of paper or on a computer screen. Different projections use varying kinds of *grid systems* to *plot* locations

Mental map – the picture of a place, its layout, and its linking routes that a person holds in his or her mind

Navigation – plotting a route and directing a ship, airplane, or other vehicle from one place to another; we now use the word to apply to journeys on foot as well

Oblique view – a view of the earth's surface from above, not looking straight down but at an angle to the surface

Observatory – a building in which *astronomers* work with telescopes and other instruments

Papyrus – the ancient Egyptian form of paper made from reeds

Parchment – animal skin stretched and cleaned to make it suitable for writing and drawing on

Petroglyph – a carving or scratching of shapes and graphical marks on stone

Plague – a deadly disease that spreads quickly among people, especially in overcrowded conditions

Plotting – making a plan or map of an area; or marking a course–of a ship or an aircraft, say–on a map

Polder – a large piece of land, surrounded by protective embankments, reclaimed from the sea by pumping out the water

Poles – the points at either end of the earth's axis of rotation where it meets the earth's surface; also called the Geographic North and South Poles

Prime Meridian – the line of *longitude* at 0 degrees; by international agreement it is the line that passes through Greenwich, London, England

Reference system – a method of recording the position of places on a map so that they all relate logically to one another. Lines of *latitude* and *longitude* make up one reference system

Relief – the shape of the earth's surface, its hills, mountains, and depressions

Sea level – the average level of the sea along the coastline; used as the zero point for measuring land heights, airplane altitude, and sea depths

Small-scale map – a map that shows a large area with only a little detail; like a *bird's-eye view* from a great distance above the earth

Soft-copy map – a map on a computer screen that is not drawn on paper and can be switched off

Surveying – the measuring of altitudes, angles, and distances on the land surface in order to obtain accurate positions of features that can be mapped. Surveying the oceans and seas also means measuring distances and angles between visible coastal positions, but the third dimension measured is depth rather than height

Symbol – a diagram, icon, letter, or character used on a map to represent a specific characteristic or feature

Terrain – the physical character of an area of land; its *relief*, vegetation, and so on

Thematic map – a map that shows one particular aspect of the natural or human environment, such as transportation routes, weather patterns, tourism, population, vegetation, or geology

Thermometer – an instrument for measuring temperature

Topographic map – a map that shows natural features such as hills, rivers, and forests, and man-made features such as roads and buildings

Vellum – a fine kind of *parchment* made from the skin of very young goats or lambs

Zero point – the point that defines the position of all other reference points on a map

Zodiac – a division of the night sky; there are 12 such areas covering the whole of the cosmos

Zoning – planning what use of land will be made, or allowed, in an area in the future

Further Reading and Websites

Barber, Peter, ed. *The Lie of the Land*, British Library Publishing, 2001

Driver, Cline *Early American Maps and Views*, University Press of Virginia, 1988

Forte, I., et al., *Map Skills and Geography: Inventive Exercises to Sharpen Skills and Raise Achievement*, Incentive Publications, 1998

Haywood, John, et al., *Atlas of World History*, Barnes & Noble Books, 2001

Letham, Lawrence *GPS Made Easy*, Rocky Mountain Books, 1998

Monmonier, Mark *How to Lie with Maps*, University of Chicago Press, 1991

Monmonier, Mark *Map Appreciation*, Prentice Hall, 1988

Meltzer, M. *Columbus and the World around Him*, Franklin Watts, 1990

Stefoff, Rebecca *Young Oxford Companion to Maps and Mapmaking*, Oxford University Press, 1995

Thrower, Norman J. W. *Maps and Civilization: Cartography in Culture and Society*, 2nd ed., University of Chicago Press, 1999

Wilford, John. N. *The Mapmakers*, Pimlico, 2002

www.auslig.gov.au/
National mapping division of Australia. Find an aerial photograph of any area of the country

http://cgdi.gc.ca/ccatlas/atlas.htm
Internet-based Canadian Communities Atlas project. Schools create their own atlas

www.earthamaps.com/
Search by place name for U.S. city maps, with zoom facility

http://earthtrends.wri.org
World Resources Institute mapping of energy resources, agriculture, forestry, government, climate, and other thematic maps

http://geography.about.com
Links to pages on cartography, historic maps, GIS, and GPS; print out blank and outline maps for study purposes

http://ihr.sas.ac.uk/maps/
History of cartography; no images, but search for links to many other cartographic topics

www.lib.utexas.edu/maps/
Vast map collection at the University of Texas, historical and modern, including maps produced by the CIA

www.lib.virginia.edu/exhibits/lewis_clark/
Information on historic expeditions, including Lewis and Clark

www.lindahall.org/pubserv/hos/stars/
Exhibition of the Golden Age of the celestial atlas, 1482–1851

www.LivGenMI.com/1895.htm
A U.S. atlas first printed in 1895. Search for your town, city, or county

http://memory.loc.gov/ammem/gmdhtml/
Map collections 1500–1999, the Library of Congress; U.S. maps, including military campaigns and exploration

www.nationalgeographic.com/education/maps_geography/
The National Geographic educational site

http://oddens.geog.uu.nl/index.html
15,500 cartographic links; search by country or keyword

www.ordsvy.gov.uk/
Site of one of the oldest national mapping agencies. Search for and download historical and modern mapping of the U.K. Go to Understand Mapping page for cartographic glossary

www.mapzone.co.uk/
Competitions and quizzes for younger readers about Great Britain; site run by Ordnance Survey

http://www.libs.uga.edu/darchive/hargrett/maps/maps.html
University of Georgia historical map collection; maps from the 16th to the early 20th century

http://topozone.com/
Search by place name or latitude and longitude for all areas of the U.S. Maps at various scales

www.un.org/Depts/Cartographic/english/htmain.htm
United Nations cartographic section. Search by country and by different UN missions worldwide

http://mapping.usgs.gov/
U.S. national atlas and much more, including satellite images

http://interactive2.usgs.gov/learningweb/students/homework_geography.asp
USGS site for students; all kinds of useful information. Create your own map by plotting latitude and longitude coordinates

www.worldatlas.com/
World atlas and lots of statistics about all countries of the world

Set Index

Numbers in **bold** in this index refer to the volume number. They are followed by the relevant page numbers. A page number in *italics* indicates an illustration.

A

Aborigines, Australian **3**: *6-7*, **5**: *25*, 37
Académie Royale des Sciences (France) **6**: 6, 8, *25*
aerial photographs
  film used for **8**: 19
  in geographic information systems **8**: 17
  mapmaking from **1**: *8-9*, 14, 30, **6**: 13, *25*, **7**: *14*, 15, *19*
  maps, comparison with **1**: *12-13*, 14
  photogrammetry **2**: 25, **6**: 13
  problems with **2**: 22, 24
  reconnaissance flying **6**: *25*, *28-29*
  from satellites **2**: 25, 29, **8**: 18
  techniques for taking **2**: *24*, 25
  used for measurement **2**: *22-25*
aerial surveying **8**: *28-29*
aeronautical charts **3**: *28-29*
Africa
  colonization **5**: 28, *29-31*
  exploration of **5**: 7, 28, *29-31*
    Landsat image of **8**: 22
  mapping of **5**: 28, *29-31*
Africa, North
  map of **1**: *30-31*
Africa, South *see* South Africa
Africa, west coast **5**: 7, 8
agricultural landscapes **1**: *13*
  see also rural areas
agrimensores (Roman surveyors) **2**: 12, **7**: 8
air traffic control systems (ATCS) **4**: 35, 36
  terminal radar approach control (TRACON) **4**: 35
  very high frequency omni-directional **4**: 35
airline maps **3**: 31
airplanes
  automatic flight logs **4**: 37
  blind flying **4**: 35
  direction-finding (D/F) aerials **4**: 36
  GPS for **3**: 28, **4**: 37
  great circle routes for **4**: *34-5*
  head-up displays (HUD) **4**: *37*
  navigation for **3**: 28-29, **4**: *34-37*
  reconnaissance flights **6**: *25*, *28-29*
  solo long-distance flights **4**: 36
  spy planes **6**: *25*, 28, 29, **8**: *21-22*
Alexander VI, Pope **5**: 17
Alexander the Great **6**: *22-23*
Alexandria, Egypt **7**: 9

alidades **2**: 18
altitude *see* elevation
Amazon River **5**: 8
America, Central
  early cities **7**: 7
America, North
  colonial maps **5**: *20-23*, 25
  continental divide **5**: 23
  exploration of **5**: *22-23*, 25
  indigenous peoples **3**: 11, **5**: 16, 19, *21-23*, 25
  Louisiana territory **5**: 22, 25
  maps of **1**: *34-35*, **2**: *32-33*, **5**: *11*, *22*, *23*, 25
  see also individual areas/cities/states; Canada
America, South **4**: 16, **5**: 8, 32
  early cities **7**: 7
  maps of **3**: *11*, **5**: 11
  see also individual countries
American-Canadian border **5**: *32-33*
American Civil War (1861-65) **6**: *22*, 31
the Americas
  discovery of **1**: *28*, **4**: 14, *15-16*, **5**: *8-10*
  first use of name **5**: 9
  indigenous peoples **5**: 16
  maps of **1**: *28*, **5**: 6, *10-11*
  observatories **1**: *24-25*
animals, navigational abilities **3**: *34-37*, *36-37*
Mt. Annapurna II, Nepal **5**: *26*
angles, measurement of **2**: 10, *11*, 12, 13, 15, *16*, *18-21*, **4**: 8, 9
Antarctic Circle **4**: 23
Antarctica **5**: *16*, 35
Antwerp, Netherlands **5**: 12
Arab traders **4**: *12-13*
archaeology **6**: 16
  radar applications for **8**: 29
Arctic Ocean **4**: 23
area measurement **3**: 21
Argentina **5**: 8
Asia **5**: 9
  map of **5**: *15*
  see also individual countries
astrolabes **4**: 8, *8*, 9, 13
astronomical maps **1**: 21, **8**: *24-27*
  the celestial globe **8**: *26-27*
  creation myths **1**: 21, *22-24*, 26
  Earth depicted on **1**: 22, 24, 25
  history of **1**, *22-26*
  for navigation **4**, 6, 7
  from observations **1**: *21-25*, *26*
  of planets **1**: 35
  as views from below **1**: 8
  see also planets; space
astronomical observations **1**: *24-25*, **8**: 25
  in Egypt **1**: *26*
  in Greece **1**: 28
  in India **1**: *24*

mapmaking from **2**: 6, 7, **5**: 7, 6: 9
  planetary **1**: 35, **4**: 22
  see also stars
Athens, Greece **7**: *25*, 36
Atlantic crossings **3**: 13
Atlantic Ocean **4**: 23, **5**, 8, 10, 17
  maps of **3**: *11*
atlases **5**: 13, 26, **7**: 13
  derivation of name **6**: 14
  national **6**: 6, 9, 14, *15*
  see also maps
atomic clocks **4**: 30
attributes, mapping of **2**: *31*, **8**: 12
Australia
  Aboriginal people **3**: *6-7*, **5**: *25*, 37
  Ayers Rock (Uluru) **5**: 37
  as a colony **5**: 36, 37
  discovery of **4**: 22, **5**: 17
  exploration of **3**, 7, **5**: 25
  geological surveys **6**: 16
  maps of **3**: 6, **4**: 23, **5**: *24*, 25
  mineral resources **6**: 16
  national mapping agency (AUSLIG) **6**: 13
  satellite image of **8**: *29*
  Sydney **6**: 19
Australian Antarctic Territory **5**: 16
AWACS (Airborne Warning and Control System) airplanes **6**: 30
axonometric maps **7**: *18-19*
Aztecs, route maps by **3**: 10

B

Bahamas, discovery of **4**: 14, 15, 16
balloons, surveillance from **6**: 29
bathymetric charts **1**: 35, **2**: 10, **3**: 28
  see also hydrographic charts
bearings **2**: 18
bees *see* honeybees
Behaim, Martin **4**: 17
Belgian colonies **5**: 31
below the surface features **1**: *34-5*, **6**: 16, *17*
  underground railways **7**: 34, 35
  see also geological maps
Bengal, India **5**: 26
Berlin Wall **5**: 34
Berlin West Africa Conference (1884-85) **5**: 28, 31
Bighorn River, Wyoming, Landsat image of **8**: *28*
birds
  navigational abilities **3**: *34*, *35*, 36
  as navigational aids **4**: 13
bird's-eye-views **1**: 8, 9, 10, *11*, 30, **7**: *12*, 13
  see also maps
Birtles, Francis **3**: 7
Bismark, Otto von **5**: *28*

Blaeu, Willem Janszoon **5**: *14-15*
Board of Longitude (Britain) **4**: 21
Boeing A-3 Sentry **6**: 30
Bolivia **5**: 32
Bollman, Hermann **7**: *18-19*
Bombay, India **7**, *26-27*
Bonne map projection **2**: 36, 37
"Bonnie Prince Charlie" (Charles Edward Stuart) **6**: 6
Booth, Charles **7**: *22-23*
  Life and Labour of the People of London **7**: 22, 23
  his poverty maps **7**: *22-23*
borders **5**: 31, 32, *33-35*, **6**: 37
  as artificial **5**: 19
  disputes over **5**: 32, 33-34
  effect of introducing **5**: 19
  fortified/defended **5**: *33-34*
  national **5**: 32, *33-35*
  property boundaries **5**: *34-35*
Bosnia **6**: 35, 36
boundaries *see* borders
boundary markers **1**: 21, 26, 35
  national boundaries **5**: *33-34*
Brazil
  Brasilia **7**: 29
  discovery of **5**: 8, 17
  Landsat image of **8**: *23*
British colonies **5**: 16, 17, 28, *31*
  in North America **6**: 27
  see also America, North; Australia; India
British East India Company **5**: 26
Buddhist world map **1**: *25*
Buenos Aires, Argentina **5**: 19
Burgess, Ernest W.
  his land use model **7**: *30*, *31-32*
Burke, Robert **5**: *24*, 25

C

Cabot, John **5**: *9-10*
Cabral, Pedro **5**: 8
cadastral mapping **6**: *7*, **7**: 9
  of property boundaries **5**: *34-35*
cairns **3**: *16*
Cairo, Egypt **7**: *25*
Canada
  American border **5**: *32-33*
  Center for Topographic Information **6**: 10, 12
  exploration of **5**: *9-10*
  French colonies **5**: 21
  mapping of **5**: 6, *11*, **6**: 13
  mineral resources **6**: 12
  national atlas **6**: 11
  stone carvings **1**: 21
canals **7**: *26*
Cantino, Alberto, duke of Ferrara **5**: 11
Cape of Good Hope **5**: 8
Cape Town, South Africa **5**: 19
capital cities **7**: *26-27*
car information systems *see* in-car information systems

Picture Credits

Abbreviations:
AAA   Ancient Art & Architecture Collection
C   Corbis

Jacket images Oblique view of antique map (background), Ken Reid/Telegraph Colour Library/Getty Images;
T-in-O map of the world drawn in 1450 (inset, top), AKG London; three-dimensional map of the topography of
Mars (inset, bottom), NASA/Science Photo Library. **6** NASA; **7** U.S. Geological Survey; **8** Kevin Fleming/C; **10-11**
Bob Rowan; Progressive Image/C; **12, 13l** University of Newcastle; **13r** Centre Nationale d'Etudes Spatiale,
France/University of Newcastle; **18** AAA; **19l** Metropolitan Transportation Authority; **19r** Gianni Dagli Orti/C;
21l Societa Cooperativa Archeologica le Orme dell' Uomo; **21r** Werner Forman Archive; **22** R. Sheridan/AAA;
23 AAA; **24l** Jeremy Horner/C; **24r** Arvind Garg/C; **25** Spink & Son, London/Werner Forman Archive; **26**
Science Photo Library; **27** Gianni Dagli Orti/C; **28** R. Sheridan/AAA; **29** C; **30-31** R. Sheridan/AAA; **31** C; **32l**
U.S. Geological Survey; **32r** Trails Illustrated/U.S. Geological Survey; **36** Gianni Dagli Orti/C.